INTRODUCTION

I've always felt sorry for the Biblical Job.

I mean, there he is, enjoying a very nice life which, from what we can see, he's worked hard for. He's got a large, seemingly loving family, servants who appear to respect him, and plenty of money. He seems happy, successful, and honourable, by all accounts.

Then, one day, Satan gets bored, goes for a stroll around Earth, and happens across Job, a good, faithful and observant Jewish man, who loves his God, and keeps the various commandments and religious requirements of his faith without complaint. This irritates Satan, who, like most of us, doesn't care much for goody-two-shoes.

Satan turns up in the heavenly realm with some other angels. You can imagine how that would've played out: these other angels side-eyeing him, moving as far away from him as possible, and muttering darkly about the nerve of the traitorous so-and-so.

God, after a somewhat ennui-laden demand that Satan explain what he's doing there and what he's been up to, asks if Satan has noticed Job. Job, God says, is wonderful, an example among men, etc, etc. (It tends to get somewhat tedious when divine beings parade their mortal pets.)

Satan smugly replies that Job is only so reverential of God because he enjoys a very comfortable life. In Satan's own words - "Take from him his wealth and comforts, and he will curse you to your face."

God, having a strange idea of how to behave towards people who've been nothing but dutiful and respectful in their dealings with you, shrugs, and responds:

"Do what you want to Job, but you can't kill him."

And off Satan goes, to begin making Job's life a complete misery, including killing his entire family and all his livestock, making him homeless, and inflicting him with leprosy, all because a God and a fallen angel were lazily shooting the breeze, and, well... Mortals don't matter, do they?

Being unemployed in the UK and reliant on government welfare provision, whilst trying to find a job that will pay you a decent wage and doesn't require you to move halfway across the country (which, if the only income you've had to date has been welfare, you won't be able to afford to do anyway), or sell a kidney to afford the travel costs associated with actually *being* employed, most places now being packed with houses, and shops offering part-time, zero-hours contracts, rather than full time employment with full time wages, is a little like being Job: You've not really done anything wrong other than manage, through no fault of your own, to attract the attention of some rather sadistic individuals who've decided that your life could be a good basis for a particularly vicious experiment. Like Job, it doesn't matter what happens to you so long as you don't die – because explaining deaths to the various pesky agencies who start sticking their noses in when a particular group of people starts to experience a large number of unexpected deaths is tiresome when you're the government, rather than an actual god.

And, just like poor old Job of Biblical fame, you'll inevitably have "well-meaning friends" show up and go on and on about how everything that's happened to you is actually your fault. These days, though, they're not just your friends, and they're not just talking to you: they're screaming about what a terrible excuse for a human being you are, how you're the only one to blame for your predicament, how you must have done something to bring this on yourself, from the lofty heights of government, the media, corner-office level business. Anyone who's supposed to help and support you is likely to try and blame you.

Defeating Worrisome Predators can best be viewed as a field guide, discussing what's likely to happen to you should you find yourself without recognised employment, and require financial assistance from the welfare state – a state which is no longer particularly interested in your welfare – in order to meet the financial burdens of staying alive long enough to make alternative arrangements to secure fiscal advantage.

It will also give you some ideas of how to avoid the worst of the government's wrath, until such a time as you're beyond their remit, either because you've managed to obtain full time, paid employment, you've reached retirement age, or you've died.

I've come through this particular battle alive, and mostly in one piece. People paying me for the work I do on a self-employed basis has promoted me away from the front line, but the fact that I don't yet earn enough to pay tax, combined with the ad-hoc nature of self-employment, and the fact that the medical condition that saw me firstly dismissed from a job, and, following that, unable to convince anyone else to take me on as a member of staff, is of the type that isn't going to go away, and will always hold a certain amount of sway over my lived experience and abilities, means I will never be entirely off the field.

This book is for those still on the front lines, my fellow field officers, and all those who will undoubtedly be deployed in the future. I can't do much, but I hope I can offer some small measure of comfort through these pages.

I hope this book helps. If the words don't, it may make a good fly swatter. It should also burn quite well, if you find yourself at a loss for heating. (That's happened to me on more than one occasion. I managed without burning books, but only just.)

Stay safe out there, and remember: This, too, shall pass.

JOBLOTS AND DISCONTENTS

Of course, it's a well-known fact that there's plenty of jobs out there. Those elements of the British workplace that are unemployed are simply feckless, apathetic, lazy. They've got no initiative.

 (Interesting side note: I'm half Irish on my dad's side, and, every time I hear the word 'feckless', I find myself thinking, in a brogue that never gets near my physical speech: "Aye, I truly have no fecks left to give, so just feck off with yiz fecking nonsense, yiz useless fecking article." Fortunately, this never makes it out of my head. Although I'd love to see the looks on various official faces if it ever did.)

 Of course, the commentators on the state of the nation as displayed in the unemployed must be right – just look at all the recruitment agencies! All the online jobs boards! All the newspaper vacancy listings! Just listen to all the businessmen – it usually *is* men – crying out for more staff, so they can take their business to the next level; as though employment is just another offering in the slew of computer and console games with which we foster "ADHD-lite", the socially acceptable shoulder shrug of abdicated responsibility, and the reason we can ignore actual ADHD, and those who suffer from it, with a clear conscience. So that we can encourage solitary pursuits, and then blame individuals for being socially isolated. Even if the fact is that they've actually found a society and kinship larger and more diverse than we could ever imagine through these "single player" games.

 No, the British public *are* just lazy. It's a good job, really, that after a few years of dossing about during the recession of the 1920s-1930s that they got their act together and roused themselves in time for the Second World War, isn't it?

 The thing about jobs is, they're not tins of baked beans. You can't just stroll along, chucking likely-looking jobs with a decent salary into your trolley along with the bread and milk, and the cheesecake you picked up because it was on special offer.

You have to apply for these jobs. And the application process is basically a human steeplechase, with hurdles and obstacles littered along the track, for the simple reason that other human beings enjoy seeing sentient creatures fall and hurt themselves.

The bloodlust of our base ferocity is never far from the surface. The first hurdle is that employers never, ever tell you what they actually *want*. This is usually because they know damn well that they can"t *afford* what they actually want. They complicate this first hurdle by believing that they, and, by extension, any job they offer, must be complex, engaging, and thoroughly fascinating. So, rather than saying for example, *"We need someone to do the boring jobs in an office. You'll mostly be sitting in front of a computer, waiting for the phone to ring. Every so often, you'll be barked at to do some photocopying, or go and make cups of tea"*, you'll see adverts saying things like:

"We are looking for an engaging, efficient face of a dynamic, forward-thinking company. You will be the first impression our customers receive of the company, and responsible for directing queries to the appropriate department, so that they can be actioned promptly. You will assist colleagues and senior staff with vital elements of their jobs, and work with them to build a cohesive, committed culture. You will be a competent user of Microsoft Office, including Excel, have some familiarity with Sage Line 50, and be experienced in all aspects of high-level professional office procedures. 6 miles NE of Norwich."

Of course, the former description encourages you to think "Hell, yeah, I could do that – especially for £270 a week" (full time minimum-wage in the UK), while the latter makes you think "Agh, I'm not sure whether I'd be good enough for that. And I'm not that good with computers and that." Especially if you've been out of work for a long time, and have started to believe the negative publicity that's churned out on a daily basis about the long-term unemployed.

And, if you were paying attention, you'll have spotted the next hurdle: no one ever tells you where they, and the job they're offering, actually is. "Six miles North East of Norwich" could be anywhere. And buses probably don't run there from where you live. And, if you don't have a car (which, let's face it, you may not do, cars being expensive, and welfare payments not being overly generous), the DWP will fine (sorry, sanction) you for "refusal to apply for a job." Because, of course, you have to identify a "legitimate" reason why you would be unable to consider a job *in advance* of contacting the employer. There is, of course, always the fact that the DWP may not consider "I can't get there, because it's 30 miles from where I live, there are no buses, and I don't have a car" a "legitimate" reason.

If you successfully navigate these hurdles, decipher the job advert, and work out that you'd be able to get there and back at the times you'd be required from and to, you meet the next hurdle: the applicant tracking system.

In plain English – a computer scans your application form and CV, and decides whether you meet enough of the keywords the employer has decided relate to the job they're advertising.

Don't know about keywords? I'm not surprised. I know about keywords because I'm paid to know about them. Basically, keywords are terms that are designed to "tell" a computer that it's found what it's looking for.

Keywords are what search engines like Google use to populate their results. With the applicant tracking system, the keywords are used to identify the closest-matching application forms.

The problem is, employers never tell you what keywords they're using. You have to guess. And if you're applying for a job in a sector that you've not worked in before, or you've been out of work for a long while, and everything's moved on, you're not likely to be able to guess enough of them to get past the applicant tracking system hurdle.

But, potentially, you can clear this hurdle, too. You'll hear those words guaranteed to lift your heart: "We'd like to offer you an interview."

Home strait, right?

Not quite – because prospective employers aren't the only ones setting up hurdles.

If your interview clashes with a Jobcentre appointment, you're expected to reschedule the interview.

Yes, you read that right – the DWP consider it *more important* that you turn up and talk to them about why you don't have a job than that you attend an interview that might get you a job, and out of their hair.

On one memorable occasion, I had an interview in Thetford, which was 30 miles from where I was living. I'm medically banned from driving, so getting to Thetford from Shipdham involved taking a bus from Shipdham to Dereham, another bus from Dereham to Norwich, then a train from Norwich to Thetford, as, at that time, no buses ran from my part of Norfolk to Thetford.

I phoned the Jobcentre, and explained that I wouldn't be able to make my signing appointment, and it had been made clear that the employer was looking to hire quickly, and so was unlikely to be able to reschedule the interview. I was asked what time I expected to be back in Dereham (where my local Jobcentre was.) I told them I should be back by 3.30-4pm. It was agreed that I would come in and sign on at 4pm.

I went to the interview. It seemed to go okay. Then the train back was late. And then failed to arrive entirely. I phoned the Jobcentre from the station, and was told there was nothing they could do. I asked if I could sign on in Thetford or Norwich. No, I had to sign at Dereham.

When a train finally turned up, I phoned the Jobcentre again, and told them I would probably be back by 5pm – to be told "We close at 5pm. If you're not here by ten-to, you'll be sanctioned for a missed signing appointment." I asked again if I could sign in Norwich. Again, I was told I had to sign in Dereham.

I called the Jobcentre as the bus from Norwich to Dereham was coming in to Dereham, at exactly 4.50pm. I explained it would take me ten minutes to get from the bus stop to the Jobcentre, to which I was told "If the doors are locked, you'll have missed your signing appointment, and will be sanctioned."

The doors were locked when I got in. Two days later, I got a letter of sanction in the post – dated the day of the interview. The day I'd spent using my mobile phone credit to desperately try and rearrange things.

I didn't get the job, either.

You'll also have to make sure you can actually afford to get to the interview – because the Jobcentre will kick up merry hell about paying for your travel if you can't. You're told to "explain to the employer", that they'll "understand."

On the one occasion I wasn't able to afford to get to an interview, the employer *didn't* understand. Not only was I sworn at and verbally abused over the phone – I got sanctioned for failure to attend.

I had no one I was able to ask to lend me bus fare. No one who was able – or willing – to give me a lift. The Jobcentre had refused to help with bus fare, telling me I "must" have family or friends who could help.

That's another thing that no one talks about: long term unemployment, and the poverty it inevitably brings with it, will make it abundantly clear who your friends are.

I found out I had one – yes, **one** friend – who stuck with me. Everyone else slowly stopped talking to me. Slowly stopped bothering to interact with me at all. Slowly started avoiding me. I stopped being told about things that were happening, stopped being invited places.

I became a social leper – as though joblessness was contagious. If you successfully navigate all these hurdles, and actually get to interview – there's another hurdle waiting for you: the fact that you don't get a second chance to make a first impression.

And, in employment, the right first impression involves looking like you've just stepped out of a high end catalogue. Right clothes, right skin, right hair style. Right make up, if you're a woman. All things that don't usually fall within the budget of welfare payments.

You need to have the right accent – not too posh, not too chavvy. You need to seem competently intelligent, but not as though you live in an ivory tower.

Hurdles, hurdles, everywhere. You're lucky if you make it this far.

IMPRESSIONS, IMPORTANCE & IMPROVEMENTS

The DWP, when you attend one of their "work-readiness" courses – where you will learn such mind-shattering things as 'wear clean clothes to interviews', 'brush your teeth', 'shave (if relevant)', 'shower', and other wondrous things – you will be given the impression that finding employment is a kind of science: Add a dash of ingredient X to mixture Y, and success is inevitable.

Those who work at the DWP ought to spend more time working with scientists. If they did, they would come to understand that nothing is "inevitable", it is only ever "in accordance with the stated hypothesis." And science also acknowledges that hypotheses will not necessarily be confirmed. They may be disproved. Science is, in fact, much more closely aligned with the arts than it might care to admit. The arts acknowledges the existence of infinite unknown and unknowable variables.

In the ocean of first impressions, the most important of these variables is the mood of the person you're trying to impress.

Get an interviewer who got out of bed the wrong side that morning, or who doesn't like the type of person you happen to be, whose cat ignored them when they wanted a warm, furry cuddle, and it doesn't matter how good you look, how well prepared or well qualified – you probably won't be getting the job.

You might say "they should know better", and I'd be inclined to agree with you. At the very least, they should *behave* better. The rest of us do, after all. I've gone into work, and did my job well, the morning after I'd attempted suicide. It is eminently possible to be dispassionate, open, and focused on your work when you're feeling down. It's what most people call "being professional."

What you have to remember, however, is that, once you reach the kind of point where you have significant responsibility, you don't have to be professional any more. "Being professional" is simply part and parcel of the begging-bowl of trying to secure firstly employment, and, once you've succeeded with that, advancement.

A second unknown variable is *the person you'll be replacing*. If the company is sorry to be losing them, they're not going to hire you unless you're exactly like them. By contrast, if they had a hard time with the person, you won't get the job unless you're *nothing* like the previous person.

You don't know the person you're replacing, nine times out of ten, so you can't possibly hope to convince the employer that you're the perfect replacement.

And then there's the fact that technology is now in play. Not in the sense of the expectation that you'll know how to use it, but in the sense that employers with certain prejudices and preconceptions can easily indulge them.

I once worked for a manager who insisted on looking up potential applicants' addresses on Google street view. She didn't like hiring people who lived in council flats - "they're usually lazy and scruffy, and won't hang around much after their first pay packet", nor did she want to hire people from "too nice" areas - "they don't need the job, do they? They're not going to stick around." I had been fortunate in that, at the time I'd applied for the job, I was living with my parents, who lived in an old, faded bungalow in a rural backwater. Not too "nice", not too run down, either.

Quite apart from street view, there's Google itself. If you have a computer with the internet near at hand, type your own name into Google, and see what comes up. Because, have no doubt about it, that's the first thing any employer who shortlists you for interview will do.

My results all relate to my writing work, with the first-displayed photo results being either shots from my wedding, or photographs I've taken.

The good thing about this particular hurdle is you can jump it, or at least, work around it. Start a blog. Get a social media presence going. Make sure you tag yourself in photographs and blog posts that represent you well. Control the conversation that's inevitably going to be going on about you among the people who will be deciding your future.

You can also prepare to make the best, closest-matching impression on those members of the company you're being interviewed by who will be deciding whether you're hired or not. Do deep background, not just on the company you have an interview with, but also on the specific department you might be working in, and, if possible, on the people you'll be reporting to, and working with. This is relatively easy; the business-focused social network LinkedIn has a lot of useful information, and gives a better sense of the individual than does a corporate website's personnel page. If you don't feel like signing up to LinkedIn (it's free), a simple Google search will be a good start. Find out what kind of people the company employs. Find out how the company sees itself, and think about how you can tailor your genuine self, skills, and interests to best resemble that image.

When you are in receipt of welfare payments, it is important to keep detailed records of the advertisements for each of the jobs you apply for – ideally, keep copies of the actual job advertisements themselves. Alongside each advertisement, make notes outlining how you match the qualities or skills mentioned in the advertisement.

Your job, whilst in receipt of welfare, is to stay alive. It annoys the government that people who are "economically inactive" are protected from being euthanised. The government likes free market capitalism – it likes it very much – but it doesn't like the necessary fact of free market capitalism, that there must always be a pool of the economically inactive, as an effective way to dissuade the currently employed from complaining about their lot. What the government really wants is to have free market capitalism without the required side effect. While the government can make your life a misery, they can't kill you. The UK government is like Satan, while the unemployed are Job: they can do anything they like to you, but they can't actually kill you.

In America, there is a long history of "suicide by cop": it may one day be the case that, in the UK, we find ourselves faced with "suicide by government" - if you're feeling particularly desperate, all you need do is ensure you end up unemployed, and the situation will resolve itself soon enough. We're not there yet, of

course, but it's looking increasingly like a potential possibility.
For now, though, focus on staying alive in spite of the
government. Pre-empt their attempts to deny you the small
amount of money you rely on to keep body and soul together.

So, how do you launch a pre-emptive strike against the massed
ranks of the UK government? That's where a process I call
"creative negativity" comes in. You don't look at the positives, at
the skills, knowledge and experience you have, at the reasons you
would be an asset to an employer. Instead, you look at, and list, all
the reasons you wouldn't be hired. All the things you can't do. All
the skills you haven't acquired. All the experience you don't have.
You write down everything you've ever got wrong, every failure
you've ever experienced. Look them full in the face. Examine
them, inside and out, until you understand exactly why they
happened, and how you could prevent them, or something like
them, happening in the future. After every interview rejection,
write down everything that went wrong, and what you could do
about it.

Present this list to your advisor. Draw their attention to those
areas where you have no influence, but where the Jobcentre may
be able to offer support and assistance.

When you lay your flaws out in front of someone, you rob them
of any power to criticise you. They are obliged to help you,
because you have made it clear that you don't have the ability or
resources to address the issues you've identified yourself. If you
weren't interested in improving yourself and your prospects, you
wouldn't be drawing attention to your failings, would you?

Creative negativity can also help you prepare for interviews.
Write down every reason you can think of that would mean you'd
be rejected. Write down every weakness in your application. Write
down every time you've failed or been rejected in something like
this particular interview. Then look at your list. Identify the issues
you can do things about for yourself. Then identify the issues you
can do things about for yourself with help from others. Finally,
identify the issues you need third parties to address for you.

Ignore all except the first group of issues – those you yourself can address. The other issues can be resolved in time.

 If one of the ways you've identified of addressing a weakness is "gain more qualifications", then it's worth looking into sites such as futurelearn.com, where a wide-variety of university-accredited short courses are available for free. You can follow the courses online, and complete them in your own time.

A CREATIVELY NEGATIVE INTERLUDE:
The supposed reasons for unemployment.
Looking through those thorns.
The roses behind the thorns.

For those who have never known long term unemployment, it can be utterly baffling as to how someone could be out of work for more than, say, a month at most. There *must* be something wrong with these people, some reason which is entirely within their control and capacity to change, that has meant they haven't achieved the status of "gainfully employed" yet. There must be something they're doing, or not doing, that means that, at the end of the day, the situation is their fault.

When you *are* long term unemployed, you are acutely aware that you are doing everything you possibly can to turn the situation around, to get back into work – perhaps to get work for the first time. You've made every change, taken every initiative and new action, that you can. This situation isn't your fault.

You're also acutely aware that none of this changes the fact that you feel as though you're to blame. None of it changes the fact that everyone insists it *is* your fault, from the government, through the media, to your friends and family.

The first thing you need to do in order to solve any problem is to understand what caused it in the first place. From plumbing to unemployment, simply shrugging and saying "it's not working" doesn't get you anywhere. There's always a reason something doesn't work, a reason it went wrong.

Creative negativity is about focusing on what's *wrong* in order to put things right. It's about looking for, and at, the negative in the situation in order to see the positive actions that could be taken to resolve it. It's about reaching through the thorns to get hold of the roses.

This chapter follows a very "short and simple" format – the way a mechanic might approach repairing your car, if they were to write down their thought processes. Hopefully, this will make it easier for you to translate those thought processes to your life and circumstances.

Creative negativity is a very versatile way of addressing a variety of problems – not just unemployment, although it is unemployment we'll be using creative negativity on in this chapter.

Problem One: I am unemployed
.What does this mean?
     . I am not being paid for work
     . I do not have a job
     . I am reliant on others
     . I do not have a role in life
     . I feel that others are judging me unfairly
.Why is this a problem?
     . I need money to pay my bills
     . A job, as well as providing an income, gives me a focus and a sense of purpose.
     . Not being self-reliant makes me feel anxious and unsafe, as any support I have could easily be taken away, leaving me vulnerable.
     . An identity others have conferred on me, and that I have accepted, provides me with an external focus and sense of purpose and achievement.
     . I do a lot that I am not paid for, and the judgement over the fact that I am unemployed negates all of this, and implies that I am lazy, and unconcerned about others, which is not the case.
.Which of these are aspects that I, personally, without external help, can address and/or change?
     .I probably have skills that people would pay me for. Even if I'm not able to earn enough to pay all my bills, I should at least be able to pay some of them.
Such skills might include: cleaning, dog walking, gardening, DIY, car washing, providing "man with a van" services, ironing, proofreading, writing.

.Putting the word out that I am offering these services will also address the issue of my feeling judged, as people will become aware that I am attempting to change the situation.

In order to claim Universal Credit (which is replacing all welfare payments for new claimants), you have to be available for work, working fewer than sixteen hours a week and earning under £110. This means that you could do a couple of hours work a day, at £10 an hour, and have £100 in addition to your UC payments. £100 a week will buy groceries for two people, put sufficient credit on prepayment gas and electric meters to meet most household usage costs, and pay the average water bill.

The other benefit to doing odd jobs for cash is that those odd jobs translate to skills you can list on your CV. Dog walking, for example, can be related to a potential employer as "Controlled diverse personalities with competing priorities, and led them as a unified group towards a common goal." Cleaning and gardening could be examples of "meeting and exceeding client expectations on time and in budget."

Of course, simply being unemployed isn't the only problem you'll face. The other problems that unemployment presents you with will vary from person to person, but may include things like:

.I   feel as though I'm a burden

.I feel that I am unfairly costing the tax payer money that could be better spent, for example, on the NHS

. I am unhappy having "nothing to do"

. I am in debt – without a job, I could lose my house.

All of these problems can be addressed with creative negativity, just as we addressed the main problem of unemployment. You state the problem. You state what the problem means *to you*, and you state *why* it is a problem: you list every answer you can think of, from the sublime to the ridiculous. Don't worry about putting down a "daft" response – you're the only person who's ever going to see this.

Once you have your list, once you've exhausted your brain's store of problems and issues, you go through the list, and identify the things you, personally, can do something about. You don't have to be able to completely solve the problem – there just need to be steps you can see that you could take right now, from the position you're currently in.

You focus on those things, on those steps. For now, that's enough. You've reached through the thorns, and started to brush the roses.

I do feel it is important to address the issue of being in debt, and particularly facing the loss of your home. I grew up with parents who were in debt - my father had experienced a prolonged spell of unemployment after the company he was working for folded, and my mother spent most of her life unable to hold down more than part-time work because of mental health issues. When I was thirteen, I had to attend a meeting with both my parents and their bank manager, and sign documents stating that I relinquished any claim on my parents' house in the event of their death. My father's life insurance wouldn't, at that point, have been enough to clear the mortgage. My mother didn't have life insurance. As an adult, while I've never been in debt, I've faced the prospect of losing my home because I couldn't pay the rent, and, latterly, having been able to buy my own home, the prospect of losing that because my only option in terms of getting sufficient money was selling up. (I was fortunate, in a terrible way – my father died, aged 61, from cancer related to exposure to asbestos. My mother was able to pursue a claim for compensation. She gave me a third of the money she was awarded, which enabled me to buy the house I'm now living in outright – I'd never have got a mortgage. I wouldn't have chosen to live where I do now, but it was affordable. It was better than being homeless.) When you're in that situation, whether through debt or simply not having enough money to keep going – **talk to people**. Talk to your landlord. Talk to your mortgage lender. Talk to your creditors. Problems never get solved in silence.

And yes, sadly, you might lose your home – I had to give up a rented property because I didn't have enough money to pay the rent, and the landlord wouldn't accept housing benefit. I couldn't get another property in that area because no landlords took housing benefit, and I wasn't eligible for social housing. I ended up homeless, living in a caravan without heating or running water while I waited for the money that society told me would replace my father to be paid. (For reasons I'm not going to bore you with, I couldn't live with my mother. Partly, these reasons included the fact that I was living with my fiancee, and neither of our parents would take both of us – if we weren't living together, we wouldn't have received enough money from individual welfare claims to visit one another regularly, as our families weren't local. This wasn't the whole of the reason we couldn't just move back with one or other of our parents, but the other aspects are personal, and private.) I'm now in the situation where my house isn't worth enough to buy me anywhere else – a fairly common problem when you're forced to buy dirt-cheap property, and have no money for improvements beyond a lick of paint. We're currently making do with a blocked toilet, and no heating or hot water – we've tried to sort out both the toilet and the boiler ourselves, by various means, to no avail, and we can't afford to have anyone in to look at them, never mind repair them. My wife's father is terminally ill, in a care home, so can't help. Neither of us have anyone else – no friends or other family who have the necessary skills. I do know what it's like. The fear. The frustration. The anger – at yourself, at employers, at the government, at other people, "normal" people, who use credit cards for luxuries like holidays, while you've got no means of sorting out the very basic stuff in your life.

We've taken a brief glance at the "problem" of unemployment – let's look, now, at some of the "reasons" people (usually those who *aren't* unemployed) will give for long term unemployment, and address their "thorns" - the ignorance that underpins the reasoning, and why unemployment, despite what others may tell you, isn't your fault.

Reason: People are unemployed because they lack the skills, knowledge, and experience that employers want. If they were just better educated, they wouldn't be unemployed.

You can't anticipate what skills and experience employers want – mainly because they never actually come out and *say* what they want. They'll go on endlessly about "the skills shortage", but very few of them invest in affordable, accessible training. Yes, you can usually work out what sort of knowledge a particular sector requires, and you can work on acquiring that, either via the internet, including looking into free online courses with companies like FutureLearn, or using books and magazines available at your local library. The internet is a better option, as there's a greater variety of resources available, and you can easily get in touch with people who have actually worked in the sector/s you're looking in to.

 In the UK, education is woefully behind the times. We're still fundamentally educating young people in the Victorian fashion – when the wealthy would become adults able to do as they liked, and all that was required of the poor was that they could read, write, do some basic mathematics, and stand in line and follow instructions. Education doesn't anticipate future requirements – it follows a set pattern, and the personal agenda and prejudices of whomever happens to be Minister for Education at the any given point, and reacts – late – to emerging requirements. (The internet was first launched in 1991. Ten years later, my high school finally started teaching "internet basics" as part of their ICT syllabus (Information and Computer Technology.) Even then, we didn't learn anything beyond "Here is how to set up an email account. This is how you run an internet search." (We were using Ask Jeeves at the time...) Schools are only now being instructed to teach coding – when the internet, and technology in general, is moving overwhelmingly towards open source, and most computer programmes are pre-installed, meaning that non-IT employees don't actually have to use any coding at all.

 What would have been handy, for me, would have been to be

taught the various formulae for MS Excel. But that wasn't considered important. Creating a basic database, we learned. Using Excel to create reports from stored data, not so much. I got sacked from an accountancy job because I used a calculator to add up columns of figures. No one had told me that you could get Excel to do that for you. No one had taught me how, and cognitive impairments related to a lifelong medical condition I have meant I couldn't "just get it" when it was explained to me. Reactivity, not anticipation.

Looking ahead, the skills I can foresee becoming necessary are electronics, and associated engineering, entrepreneurship and business studies, environmental impact awareness, budgeting, basic cookery, communication, and debating, along with mathematics (which underpins pretty much everything), and chemistry (as we will be relying more and more on created substances, including created foodstuffs.) Are these subjects being taught now, to exemplary standards? No. We're telling kids they have to read British writers, denying them access to other interpretations of the world around them at an age where that input can do most good. The teaching of Mathematics in British state schools has always been woefully inadequate. Skills such as musicianship, creative writing and thinking, artistic interpretation, are being lost as we desperately try and simply create "better factory workers", rather than acknowledging that the factories aren't there any more, and won't be coming back.

Reason: Someone ends up long-term unemployed because they don't "look professional".

Yes, some long-term unemployed people do look scruffy – but so do some gainfully employed people, on their days off. It can be hard to keep up with the latest trends, to find well-fitting, good quality clothes, and get a decent hair cut, when you have very little money. This is particularly an issue for women who find themselves out of work for a prolonged period, as women tend to be more harshly judged on their appearance.

The best thing you can do, male or female, is to go to a

department store, and try on three different styles of smart outfits. Suggestions:

Men:
1. **Suit, with a dress shirt and tie**
2. **Dress trousers, open collar dress shirt, and contrasting coloured jacket/blazer. Also see what this outfit looks like with the shirt buttoned, and a tie.**
3. **Smart jeans in black or cream (these colours only), with a shirt and contrasting-coloured waistcoat.**

Women:
1. **Skirt or trouser suit (whichever you prefer), with a plain blouse**
2. **Smart trousers or jeans in grey, black, or cream (those colours only), with a contrasting-coloured lightweight polo neck sweater**
3. **Ankle length skirt in black or grey, with a bright long-sleeved top (any style, but try and avoid overly fussy designs.)**

Try outfits with both smart boots and the more traditional brogue and leather-loafer style shoes, or slightly heeled shoes for women. Once you've identified what works best for you, do a tour of your local charity shops, and arm yourself with at least two full outfits in your chosen style. Footwear can often be found in charity shops, too, but if you can't find what you're looking for, make it a priority to save up and purchase a well-made pair of shoes from somewhere like Clarkes. It will save you money in the long run, as I've found out from personal experience. If you're able to take out a catalogue which allows for payment by instalments, this is also a good way to buy suitable shoes, and clothing, if you can't find what you're looking for in charity shops, affordably.
 If you know you'll be focusing on jobs in sectors like law and accountancy, it's worth investing in the traditional suit and tie (men), or trouser/skirt suit (women) that are often still preferred

by the established firms in those areas. You can always push the boundaries of the office dress code once you've got the job, and made it through your probation. Other sectors and industries, such as advertising, IT, and hospitality, tend to be more broad-minded about interview attire.

Personally, I find that the dress trousers-shirt-blazer combination suits me best, and also allows for the flexibility of wearing a tie or not, depending on where I'm going and whom I'm meeting. I also have a pair of burgundy brogues that I bought in a Clarkes' sale (no, I don't work for them – they just happen to be local to me), and which, from the off, were my "interviews, weddings, funerals" shoes, although I sometimes mix things up by wearing a pair of navy suede ankle boots – blue suede shoes that, so far, no one's stepped on!

The Jobcentre will often tell you that, if you're male, you should have short hair, and be clean shaven, and nothing else will do. I'm not going to tell you that, because I don't believe it. Obviously, you don't want to look like you slept rough, so make sure any facial hair you may choose to have is kept neat and tidy, and, if you do have long hair, make sure you wash it properly, and use conditioner – if you have a girlfriend, ask her for care and feeding tips for long hair: even if she doesn't have long hair herself, trust me, she'll know what you should be doing with it. I've seen people look professional and smart with long hair and a full beard, and I've seen scruffy looking people who are clean shaven with a short back and sides. Often, getting the clothing style right frames everything else perfectly.

At the end of the day, you can't predict a person's prejudice – I've encountered potential employers who've made it clear that they don't want a man on their team. (Ashley is a somewhat gender-neutral name; I now make sure to put "Mr" before my name on my CV, which saves everyone's time being wasted. Interestingly, I've had far fewer interviews since I started doing that, despite the social justice brigade howling that the opposite would, in fact, be the case...) Some people, sadly, won't want to hire a woman, or a non-white person, or someone who went to a particular university, or someone of a particular age. There are any number of reasons, beyond hair and clothing, that an employer will decide someone's face doesn't fit, and you haven't got a hope of predicting them. They'll happen, if the discrimination is blatant, you may be able to challenge it – but consider whether you want to work for someone with those attitudes in the first place.

Reason: People are unemployed because they are lazy.
This is certainly the DWP's attitude, and the reasoning behind their requirement of 40 hours of work-related activity for people receiving JSA (or, now, Universal Credit in respect of unemployment.)

Forty hours of work-related activity a week sounds like a lot. For many people, it sounds impossible. But it works out at just under six hours a day. (Remember – although the DWP don't work weekends, they expect you to spend weekends trying to find work.)

Here's an example of how you might spend your week, and still have some time to yourself:

Monday: 9am-12noon: Drop your CV round to local businesses in the sector you're interested in. Aim to visit both your nearest town and the next town along, providing these are accessible to you, and would be accessible on a regular basis.

5pm-8pm: Use the internet to look into recent developments both in the sector/s you have experience in, and those you would like to work in. Find out what sort of academic knowledge the sector leaders favour, and see if there are free online courses you could take. If there aren't, make a note of the details of other courses available in your area, including costs – when you next see your advisor, you'll show them this, and ask if they have any way of funding a relevant course.

Tuesday: 9am-12noon: Look on online jobs sites, such as Reed, Adzuna, Monster, as well as Facebook groups. Apply for

jobs in the sector/s you're primarily interested in, and related sectors (we'll be looking at how to identify related sectors in the next chapter.)
5pm-8pm: Go back to the internet jobs boards. Look at jobs that have the salary or job title you *really* want. See what sort of qualifications and experience they're typically asking for.

Wednesday: 9am-12noon: Go to your local library, take out books related to the knowledge you identified for those dream roles yesterday evening. Read the books, use the internet to see if there's any more recent publications in that sector, and also to identify free or affordable courses you could take. (Reed often have affordably-priced courses available.)
5-8pm: Spend some time on your job-related social media profiles. You should, at the very least, have a presence on LinkedIn, and your Facebook profile, if it is linked to the email address you use in job applications, and is under your full name, should be work-ready.

Thursday: 9am-12noon: Head to your nearest city, and drop your CV into businesses there. Pick one sector per week to focus on.
5-8pm: Email some speculative applications to companies you've heard of and would like to work for, but whom you haven't contacted or CV dropped yet. Go through local business directories if you're short on inspiration – or the Yellow Pages, if you have one.

Friday: 9am-12noon: Spend the morning researching emerging industries, and looking into what kind of skills and experience are typically required.
5-8pm: Contact companies involved in the emerging sectors in an informal way, but make it clear you'd like to know more about what they would need from entry-level employees.

Saturday: 9am-12noon: Take a wander round your local town, including areas you don't normally visit, and see what, if any, new businesses have opened up. Pop in to any you identify, and introduce yourself, explaining that you're looking for work, and asking if you can drop a CV over by email. If the businesses are the type that don't work weekends, make a note of their names, and see if they have an email address or a website on their signage.
5pm-8pm: Email your CV to the businesses you spoke to today (if any), and find email contacts for any that were closed, and email them.

Sunday: 9am-12noon: Go for a walk somewhere where there's likely to be people. Talk to people if they talk to you. You can describe this as "informal networking." If you have a local pub or cafe you like, finish up there – and talk to people. Bar and waiting staff often know a lot about potential employment opportunities.
5pm-8pm: Dedicate this session to Universal Jobmatch. Of course, you'll have been logging on to this at least once a day, to keep the Jobcentre happy, but this session is an exclusive-focus occasion.

In addition to all of the above, make sure you buy your local paper on the day when they run their job adverts. If you're not sure when this is, phone or email the paper directly and ask. Write down everything you do, the full details of every job you apply for, and any further education or training you identify as potentially being helpful. This way, when you see your Jobcentre advisor, you'll be going in armed. As long as you have proof that you've been doing a variety of things regularly, and for a significant period of time, that should lead you to at least get interviews, you can't be sanctioned. And, if you are sanctioned, you have evidence and grounds to appeal. And the best thing? If you follow the above schedule, with some variations to suit your situation, you still have up to five hours a day that's yours, allowing for over runs and travelling time. (You also have two hours over the 40 hour requirement, which means you have a bit of flexibility if things are thin on the ground, or you have other responsibilities to attend to.)

Reason: People are unemployed because the jobs simply aren't there.

This is probably the most accurate reason for unemployment, particularly long-term unemployment. Economically deprived areas are a reality – a reality created by central government, and systematic under-investment. Failure to replace industries that were overtaken by the relentless, ruthless march of Progress. Failure to invest in education and re- and up-skilling of people of working age. Failure to bring new investment, and retain existing employers. Massive house building, with no employment opportunities to back it up.

As outlined above, however, applying for jobs isn't the only recognised form of work-related activity. Informal networking counts. Looking into, and pursuing, training and education counts.

If your area genuinely doesn't have many jobs, look into what you would need to do to be able to move elsewhere. Apply creative negativity to the issue of moving – start with all the reasons you can't, and work your way up. Discuss this with your Jobcentre advisor – it shows that you're being realistic about the prospects of the area you live in, and are looking in to being elsewhere, somewhere where things are a little better.

PEBBLES AND RIPPLES

The DWP seem blissfully ignorant of the prevailing wisdom in recruitment, which is that focusing on a specific sector or job type tends to bring higher-quality results in a shorter space of time than the "fire enough shots at a broad enough target and you'll hit the bulls eye eventually" attitude that the DWP takes with those jobseekers whom circumstances have forced into "signing on."

If you're on JSA, or the JSA component of Universal Credit, you will be expected to apply for literally anything that is within your skill level. And your skill level is decided by the DWP, not you – if you apply for something they don't think you're qualified for, expect a sanction for "deliberately sabotaging jobseeking efforts." If you don't meet – and ideally exceed – your targets, consistently, expect a sanction. And if you don't get offered a job quickly enough? Expect bullying, harassment, and being moved to daily signings.

The DWP also don't seem to grasp that requiring someone to sign on every day, particularly if that person lives some distance from the Jobcentre and is reliant on public transport, takes a large chunk of time that the individual in question could be using to actually look for work. Of course, the DWP don't actually want you to find work – it isn't desirable for the government to have near-full employment. That, they will tell you, is communism, and we are not a communist country.

If the DWP wanted you to find a job, they would overhaul their service provision, and come up with more efficient procedures.

Recruitment professionals will tell you to go for "quality, not quantity", that it looks better if you can talk about applications you've made within the sector you're being interviewed for, or at least roles closely related to it.

The DWP tell you to "apply for as many jobs as possible – it's a numbers game."

When you play a numbers game with job applications, you hit several hurdles.

Firstly, employers talk to each other. They attend networking events, they drink in the same pubs, they play golf together. They probably have better things to talk about than interview candidates, but, if they don't, and it becomes clear that you're applying to everyone, no one will be interested, because you look as though you don't know what you want. You look feckless, a poor risk for the money any future employer will be expending taking you on.

Then, you have the fact that firing as many shots as you can doesn't instil any degree of accuracy. You never learn what it is that employers in your ideal sector are looking for, because your head is buzzing with snatches of white noise from what every employer, from every sector, has told you. You won't become aware of what courses you should be considering, what knowledge you should be acquired.

So, you need to be focusing your aim and efforts to give the right impression to potential employers, but you need to be keeping up the numbers to keep the Jobcentre off your back, and avoid a sanction, or the hassle of daily signing. How do you manage to do both?

Very simply – you think of ponds, pebbles, and ripples.

When you throw a pebble into a pond, there's the point of impact, and ripples spreading out, at ever-increasing distances, from that point.

The point of impact is your ideal job, and the ripples are jobs that are related to that – some very closely, some only tentatively. But a thread of awareness runs through all the ripples, even the ones at the very outer edge, and links back to that point of impact.

I'll give you an example, over the next few pages, for three different jobs: **Writer,   Fashion designer,** and **Accountant**

POINT OF IMPACT: WRITER

Immediate ripples (very closely related jobs)

- Copywriter
- Journalist
- Editor
- Blogger
- Ghost writer

Midpoint ripples (jobs that are still related to that of writer, but less obviously)

- Fundraising manager
- Business development manager
- Marketing manager
- Public relations

Final wave ripples (jobs linked to that of writer, but seeming very distant from it)

- Administrator
- Examination invigilator
- Business analyst
- Teaching assistant

Do you start to see how it works? We'll go through the other two jobs – fashion designer and accountant – and, by the end of this chapter, you should be able to do a "ripple chart" for yourself, for any job or sector you want to get in to.

POINT OF IMPACT: FASHION DESIGNER

Immediate ripples:

- **Fashion buyer**
- **Dressmaker/tailor**
- **Personal stylist**
- **Modelling agent**
- **In-house designer (fashion, interiors)**

Mid-point ripples:

- **Architect**
- **Clothing retail manager**
- **Interior design consultancy manager**
- **Events manager**

Final ripples:

- **Hair dresser**
- **Clothing retail assistant**
- **Graphic designer**
- **Advertising**
- **Visual merchandiser (setting up in-store displays.)**
- **Care assistant (in the closed environment of a care home, you'll quickly get a reputation for helping patients look their best!)**

POINT OF IMPACT: ACCOUNTANT

Immediate ripples:

- **Financial officer**
- **Business development manager**
- **Business analyst**
- **Bank manger**
- **Accounts department manager**
- **Accounts assistant**

Mid-point ripples:

- **Bailiff/debt collector**
- **Bank clerk**
- **Chair of governers (this sort of job is usually very much part time)**
- **Council clerk (as above)**

Final ripples:

- **Cashier**

The important thing is not to fall in to the trap of thinking you'll be doing a "final ripple" job for the rest of your life – you should, in fact, only stay in a final ripple job for two-three years. Long enough to show commitment, not long enough to become part of the furniture.

 Mid-point ripple jobs, you're aiming to stick with for between three and five years. Immediate ripple jobs are longer term – you should aim to get ten years in before you apply for jobs at your point of impact.

For the sake of argument, let's assume you're the same age as I am now – thirty. Perhaps it takes you a year to get a final ripple job. You'll be thirty-four, max, when you move on. Thirty-nine when you leave your mid-point ripple job for your immediate ripple job. Forty-nine when you finally get your point of impact job, which, with the current retirement age, you'll be doing for at least eighteen years. (Although it will probably be more like twenty by the time you've reached those dizzy heights.) You have time. And, if you have a significant amount of previous, relevant experience, or a related degree, you may be able to skip a few steps, start from a mid-point ripple, rather than a final ripple, Move more quickly.

It can seem impossible to get from unemployed and reliant on welfare to where you want to be, and it's that sense of a vast chasm that leads people into despair, depression, and, sometimes, suicide.

I hope I've shown you a way through that particular forest, drawn your attention to the stepping stones that link HERE to THERE.

If you would like me to draw a ripple chart for your ideal job, please email me on **negativesialsoacharge@gmail.com**, and I'll be only too happy to help – completely free of charge. If you run a company or organisation, please contact me to discuss introducing the concept in more depth, and training your staff in its application. There is a charge for this, the contact is the same email address as above, **negativeisalsoacharge@gmail.com**

EMPLOYABILITY

Having a disability or long term health issue is a full time job in itself, with a lot of demands, both mental and physical, made on your energy, your physical capacity, and your time – not to mention your pocket, because being disabled or chronically ill is often comes with additional costs, which will vary from person to person.

And yet, all too often, the UK government seem to think that there is "nothing wrong, really" with disabled people, that "if you can have Stephen Hawking and paralympic athletes, then anyone, with any disability, can work." But what the government, and the non-disabled public, miss, is that these individuals will need a *lot* of support and specialist care to perform as well as they do. And that simply isn't available for the overwhelming majority of disabled people, who also have to fight against employers' prejudices, inaccessible work places, and a refusal to make even basic accommodations, combined with an antiquated belief that "work" can only take place at the employers' premises, even though technology has now made it possible for most, if not all, office based jobs to be done from home.

I do not have a physical disability, but I do have a serious mental health issue, which has seen me dismissed from a job, and banned from working in an entire sector. I have schizophrenia, diagnosed in 2010. I'm on medication, and I'm following a course of Dialectical Behaviour Therapy (a more advanced version of Cognitive Behaviour Therapy, and more suited to the "serious" mental illnesses, as psychiatry likes to describe things like schizophrenia, bipolar disorder, and the personality issues. Which is a little bit crap, because depression and anxiety are hardly a walk in the park – I have those, too, depression more than anxiety, and it's 50/50 as to whether the depression and anxiety are genuinely co-morbid with the schizophrenia, or whether they are facets of it. As my psychiatrist said "All we know for certain is it's there, and we need to help you learn to manage it successfully.") I am also sole carer for my wife, who has Asperger's Syndrome and OCD, as well as being in recovery from an eating disorder and childhood abuse.

So, yeah – I'm pretty much working full time managing the two of us. But I'm one of the many people whom ESA assessors have declared "fit for work." (My wife does receive ESA, but was refused PIP, so we're in a better position than some people – just as well, as we've both been disowned by our respective parents, and have no other family or friends who are able or willing to help us out.)

The first thing I feel needs to be said is that "disabled" doesn't mean "broken." It means "prevented from fully functioning" - think about a laptop, when you switch off the wi-fi receiver. You'll get an error message: Wi-fi disabled. It doesn't mean that the wi-fi will never function again – it means that you have to take action to *allow* it to function. And that's what employers aren't doing. It's what the government is studiously avoiding *making* employers do. It's no good having a wheelchair ramp to get into a building if the office is on the third floor, and the lift isn't wide enough to accommodate a wheelchair – or is frequently out of action. And can't be used in the event of a fire.

It's all very well to say that "everyone has to muck in, and do a bit of everything", but you need to recognise that a deaf or hearing-impaired person shouldn't be expected to field phone calls. Talking about "workplace stress" is a good start, but you have to extend it to understanding that, for some people, the environment, rather than the workload, is what's causing the stress. You can't welcome someone with epilepsy on to your team, and then insist on having desks so close together that they're inevitably going to end up injuring themselves should they have a seizure, and not be able to get to an open space in time. You can't claim that you have "no problem whatever" with a blind team member bringing their guide dog to work, but then insist on a lot of visual presentations.

On an even more basic level, employers need to understand that it may well be the case that disabled people can't drive, or don't have access to a suitable vehicle – I'm medically banned from driving, and my wife has never even had driving lessons. We don't know whether her mother (who was mentally and emotionally abusive, and concealed much of my wife's medical history from her throughout her life) knows of a medical reason why my wife *can't* drive, and that's why she didn't have driving lessons at 17 (her mother was certainly able to afford to pay for them), but it's a moot point now – we can't afford to pay for her to have driving lessons. We do know she is visually impaired, not markedly, but potentially enough that she wouldn't be legally able to drive. Many disabled people have had their Mobility Scheme vehicles taken back by the government, and don't have the money to purchase an adapted car themselves.

And yet employers continue to claim that a driving licence and access to transport is "essential." The government continues to allow public transport to be privately owned, and run routes where the operators can make the most money, rather than where they are most needed. The government insists that London's public transport be subsidised, but everyone else is expected to meet ever-increasing costs out of their own pocket.

And, of course, we've had government ministers suggesting that disabled people "aren't worth" the national minimum wage.

And yet we're probably worth far more than non-disabled people, because managing our disabilities and health conditions provides us with skills and experience non-disabled might take years to acquire.

From a personal perspective, the skills that schizophrenia gives me include:

. People management – I have four distinct "individuals", or alters, in my head (my schizophrenia includes "elements of multiplicity", as my psych notes comment). One of the things I have to do, on a daily basis, is ensure that the one destructive alter is kept away from everyone else, and that the three who'll actually listen to me understand that a) there are certain situations they cannot be involved in, and b) that if they are involved in a situation when I'm not "there", so to speak, I need to be told what went on, so that I have at least some kind of memory of it.

.Resource management – the most common problem for schizophrenics isn't, actually, hallucinations or delusions. It's cognitive impairment and fluctuating energy levels. I've learned that, if I've been doing a lot of travelling, I'll be completely out of it the next day, and therefore need to arrange long journeys, visits, day trips, etc for a time when I don't have much on the following day. I am aware that certain kinds of news can send me into a tailspin, and, therefore, if I need to be functional, I'll avoid newspapers, news broadcasts, and social media for a couple of days, so that I have the energy and concentration to do what I need to do.

.Designing and implementing systems – life rapidly becomes very hectic when you can't remember what you said to someone two minutes after saying it, and when it may or may not occur to you to check diaries, etc. I've learned to keep notes as I'm conducting a conversation, store important information in several separate places, and ensure I tell my wife about things that are absolutely vital, in the hope that she will remind me. Calendars are placed where I will be unable to avoid seeing them, and my evening routine includes crossing off the day that's just happened (so I have half a chance of knowing where we are in any given month), and looking at the next day's page in my diary, to see what I have going on, and transferring that to an alarm notification on my mobile. I am currently working with a naturopathic medication regime, as the side effects of the orthodox medication I was on (a combination of Lamotrigine and Quetiapine, after Rispiridol triggered a major psychotic episode in a very public situation) made it impossible for me to manage even basic household tasks, never mind full time work; I had no energy, was constantly feeling dizzy and nauseaous, and had severe memory impairment.

Naturopathy involves working out – with help from a professional – exactly how much of any given medication you need, when you need it, and what your "variables" - the times you will need to increase your dosage, or take your medication at different times – are. For me, the variables I can predict are meetings, including interviews, people coming to the house, and travelling outside my home town. Other variables, I have to respond to as and when they happen, but in a way that ensures minimal disruption to the rest of my day.

I've also become very good at covering the fact that, in all probability, I *won't* remember someone's name, even if they only told me ten minutes ago, and I won't recognise someone's face unless I've seen that person regularly – and sometimes not even then. These, too, are useful skills to have in business. Finally, my need to complete a set lot of work before the monkeys in my brain start fiddling with switches means I have a very intense focus, can work without a break for several hours at a time (providing some idiot of a boss doesn't decide to interrupt me, and I'm allowed to unplug the phone), and will be very succinct in my written work – if I go on too long, I'll end up losing track of what I was going to say. It's part of why my books are so short.

If you're reading this and have a disability, you'll probably be able, over the course of a few hours or days, to identify the skills you have simply because they're an essential part of managing your disability or health condition – examples might include;

.Creative thinking – when you're functioning as a disabled person in a world designed by non-disabled people, you sometimes have to get creative just to get through your day. Why else would we now have assistance dogs that are trained by wheelchair users to operate an ATM?

.Determination – often, this is the only thing that gets us as disabled people *anything* we want.

.A sense of humour – absolutely vital, in my experience!

The Jobcentre will tell you to "minimise your disability". This is, in fact, the worst thing you can do. If you have a visible disability, it's impossible to convince non-disabled people that it's "not a problem, really", because they'll be focusing on how awful having your disability would be for them, and if you have a hidden disability, it will eventually make itself known, often in quite spectacular fashion, and at a *really* bad time, if you've been trying to suppress it. (Yes, I have indeed had a psychotic episode while at work. No one died, the building's still standing, and no clients ever knew about it. But I still got sacked and black listed.)

The best thing you can do, even though it may seem counter-intuitive, is to be upfront about your disability. Talk fully and openly about all the problems it causes you, and everything that makes it harder for you to function.

Why? Because business people are inherently suspicious of anything – be it a person or a process – that seems "problem free." They're certain someone, somewhere, isn't telling them something, and that makes them nasty and vindictive.

Business people *expect* problems. They're in business because people, processes, systems, machines, buildings, resources, have problems. They won't believe that you don't have any problems, but they'll appreciate the fact that you've identified your problems, and taken steps to address those that you can. You may not get a job out of your honesty and self-awareness – prejudice still exists, despite the government's claims to the contrary – but you will get a bit more respect than you might have done. And you'll have increased awareness, even if only by a single drop. Single drops have a habit of becoming large bodies of water, over time. Keep dripping.

When you minimise your disability or health problems, you come across as naïve, and lacking in self-awareness. When you put the problems of being you front and centre, you save potential employers a job. And most managers like being saved extra work – it's why they employ people, despite bitching about how much it costs to do so.

Of course, there are some disabilities and health issues that you simply can't work around. The best way to deal with getting this across to DWP assessors, if this is your situation, is to go through job vacancy advertisements, make a note of skills mentioned that your health issue or disability precludes you from ever coming close to acquiring, job roles that your disability prevents you from doing, issues around the set-up of the business premises, if you're able to (ideally) travel to the site and take photographs, or, alternatively, find photos online (try the company's website, or Google street view), of access, both directly to the building and in the surrounding area, and the internal layout. Bring in bus time tables if you don't have your own transport, or can't drive.

 If you're still refused welfare support, make sure you contact an advocacy organisation – in East Anglia, where I'm based, one of the largest such is Equal Lives. Search "disability employment advocacy" in your area to find the nearest organisation to you. Many disability advocacy organisations employ a significant number of disabled people, so don't ever worry that they "won't understand." It's part of the curse of disability and chronic ill-health – you become used to people not understanding, and assume no one ever will.

 On a final note – no matter what the DWP and their assessment organisations try and tell you, you ARE entitled to have an advocate, carer, friend, or family member present, and in the room with you, at ALL meetings and interactions. They won't be allowed to bring recording equipment in, or make notes – but you can't stop someone from making notes immediately they've left the room. Ensure they are timed and dated. If possible, photograph the notes with a digital camera that has an automatic time and date code, or store them on a device which will record the time and date. And ALWAYS request that the transcript of your interview is forwarded either to you, or to the person who helps you with correspondence. Be very firm on this – the DWP will try and refuse, but there is no reason why you shouldn't have access to that record. Above all – stay you, and stay safe.

WHAT THE GOVERNMENT THINKS

The government believes that there are thousands of jobs just waiting to be filled, and that the only reason unemployment is so high is that British workers simply "don't want" the jobs that are available. Apparently, while we're quite happy to accept the pittance that is welfare, and can happily handle the stigma of being unemployed, we think we're "too good" for the majority of jobs that are "out there." The UK government genuinely seems to believe that people have made a "deliberate lifestyle choice" to be unemployed, and reliant on welfare to survive. Recently, we've even had government ministers claim that the disabled and chronically ill have made a "lifestyle choice." That people would rather have serious medical conditions that limit their life, and their enjoyment of that life, than be healthy, well, and employed.

The UK government believes the reverse of what is actually the case: it believes that employers actually want to hire people, that they are keen to help the disabled, the young, and the long term unemployed become contributors to society once more. People, being the lazy good-for-nothings they are, simply don't want to hold down a job.

In fact, while most people want to work, most employers don't want the hassle of hiring people. Hiring staff is expensive – you have to advertise, you have to take time out of your day for interviews – it's all just too much grief, too much expense. Employers resent their staff, because those staff remind them of everything they can't do themselves. All the money they're paying, just because they're not good enough on their own.

And once you've had the expense of recruitment, you have the expense of simply *having* another staff member around the place. Quite apart from their salary, their holiday entitlement, their sick pay entitlement, their National Insurance contributions and all the other legal niceties that the Tories haven't quite managed to get rid of just yet, you have to provide them with a desk, a chair. They use the kettle, the coffee, the milk, the toilet paper – the expense of actually having people in your premises, doing work that you can't do, don't have time to do, or simply prefer not to do, is never ending. It's like having the builders in, only they never go away, and nothing ever really gets built. Oh, and of course, you have the cost of maintaining a physical building – business rates, the rent or mortgage payment, heating, lighting, insurance... It makes you wonder why so many UK employers are so averse to the idea of their staff working remotely, really. And it certainly explains why they'll jump on the opportunity to replace human beings with robots, as soon as the per unit cost of the robots falls to a level they're happy with. It's already started, the automation of the workplace: self-service checkouts, self-driving forklift trucks, automated warehousing, robots doing microsurgery in hospitals... No one's protected by class or status any more, which is an interesting and novel development. Usually, only the working class are exposed to the risk of being replaced by someone, or something, cheaper and less cost-intensive. This time, everyone's job could be taken by a robot.

Victor Meldrew being "replaced by a box" in the first episode of One Foot in the Grave (it's on YouTube, and well worth a watch) was comedy value twenty or so years ago – it's becoming reality now.

But, of course, employers won't tell the government how they really feel about employees, because then business would be kicked out of the cosy little foothold it has in the corridors of power. Tax breaks would be cancelled.

So, the lie continues that businesses want to employ workers – and British workers, at that! - but they simply can't get the staff. People don't have the right skills, the right attitudes. They just aren't interested in making a contribution any more.

In the government's eyes, businesses can do no wrong, and the business sector is very keen to keep things that way. Big business, the area of the broader business sector that benefits most from this charade, is very invested in maintaining their link to power, the influence they have over a mostly clueless government.

Next time there's a major issue being discussed in the media –

changes to the education system, for example, or welfare reforms – notice how the business sector is always flirted with for their comments, even when the issue in question has little or nothing to do with them. Notice the companies who are commentating. Google the individuals who are being interviewed, and find out just how much money they have to their name. And then understand that you're not a citizen under a democratically elected government: you're a commodity that's already been sold.

All of this may lead you to believe I'm anti-business: I'm not. I run my own business, and I know several other people who do. I'm interested in people who start with nothing, and make a success of something. What I'm against, always, is rampant profiteering, and a blindness to the fact that human beings have worth, and add value, too.

Smaller businesses are very good, in general, at treating people like, well, *people.* It's just that smaller businesses often can't afford to hire staff – most of the small business owners I know are doing at least three peoples' jobs at once, simply because they can't afford to hire more staff. And the Tories have only made employing people less affordable, with things like the Workplace Pension, etc. A good idea, but people aren't going to benefit from a Workplace Pension if providing it means workplaces simply choose not to hire full-time staff.

There was a time, relatively recently, that the government called small businesses "the backbone of the British economy." And they were right – it's small businesses that keep markets and high streets going. Markets and high streets are part of what attract people to particular areas, and sees them buy property there. People who buy property employ builders, decorators, landscape gardeners. They buy paint, sofas, TVs, freezers. They take out home insurance. Money flows freely through all spheres and levels of the economy. It's a shame, really, that the Tories seem so determined to make things impossible for small businesses.

There needs to be a radical review of which businesses and sectors are *seen*, and treated, as important, versus which truly are. There needs to be greater honesty between business and government about what is expected, and what the issues are around meeting those expectations. Big business needs to start seeing staff as an asset, rather than a liability.

And everyone needs to start paying their way, and working together to build a strong, vibrant, viable economy that draws people to Britain, and makes the people already here genuinely proud to be British.

MINDSETS, MANNERS, AND MINDING THE GAP

When you're a welfare recipient, it can be easy to feel that your life, your skills, your ambitions and dreams, no longer matter. You are constantly reminded of your incompetence. You face, daily, the disdain and contempt the gainfully employed – the "normal" people, as one Tory MP referred to them, in a Freudian slip – hold you in. Whatever you do, from whatever motivation, will be deemed wrong. If you live independently, you're a drain on housing benefit (whether or not you actually claim it – it's simply assumed you do.) If you live with your parents, you're sponging off them, and need to learn some self-respect. You're a layabout who's living off decent people who've worked hard all their lives.

Because, whether or not the retired actually *did* work – they always had gruelling, draining, physically demanding jobs whenever anyone's talking to you about them.

The one thing you can't do is allow yourself to believe all this. You can't let the lies the world tells you about yourself get into your head.

This can seem impossible, because, even though there's an army of people in your situation, in situations very like yours, and a reserve force who have been there before, and remember it, or can see it in their future, and fear it, the unemployed and disabled don't have the force of organisations like Age UK. We have no one to militantly challenge any statement about us that doesn't make it clear that we're suffering, struggling, and deserving of help and pity, and, ideally, more money. We're an army of individuals, scattered across the field of battle – and no one's raising a standard for us.

So you raise your own standards. You find a style that suits you, and looks smart, and you buy what clothes you can afford. You continue taking pride in your appearance, even if your monthly visit to the salon is now a monthly treat of some upmarket shampoo. You talk about the things you're doing with pride, and as though they are things worth doing, worth mentioning – because they are. Whether you're raising a family, keeping your home running smoothly, writing a novel, a play, or poetry, composing music and lyrics, planning to shoot a short film, or studying via a free online course, or through library books – be proud of that. It's worth every bit as much as someone else's day job.

When you're discussing poverty, unemployment, and disability online, particularly, remember to attack points, not people. Remain calm, back up statements with facts where you can, acknowledge that other people may simply have had experiences that meant they never encountered the life you're living, rather than that they are deliberately ignoring its existence. Accept that there is such as thing as working class snobbery – the refusal to wear appropriate clothing to interviews and upmarket events, the disdainful "they'll just have to take me as I am: I ain't gonna change for them." But, throughout this mild-mannered understanding, always hold your ground. We are the front line of the class war – and it is *we*. I'm standing with you and for you, and there are others. You just have to look for them, call to them. Remember: we have no flag to rally round. No one is going to raise the standard high to call us together. We have to find each other, and find our own way home.

If you are well enough to manage work, treat jobsearching the way you would a new hobby, when you're still in the stages of being in love with that hobby, wanting to spend all your spare time on it, to learn more about it, to talk to other people who have it as a hobby. It helps if you're focused on what *you* want to do, rather than what the DWP has told you you have to settle for. You have the right to have ambitions – even wild ambitions, at times. You have the right to be absurd, a fantasist, and utterly unrealistic. You, just like everyone else, have the right to dream. So dream your dreams – because, sometimes, dreams do come true.

Something that has to be addressed is the older generation, the retired. They're often, though certainly not always or exclusively, the ones criticising people who are unemployed. But rarely is this done from malice. It is, all too often, simply that these individuals can't understand how the life they experienced, often as adults, after childhoods of what we would now call deprivation or material poverty, could so quickly cease to exist. This is a generation that grew up without credit cards, overdrafts, and payday lenders – when they see people who are unemployed with new TVs, smartphones, new clothes, computers, internet access, when they see people like us going on holiday, they don't understand that it's probably being paid for with a loan, or a credit card: they assume that "things can't be all that bad, if you can afford all that", because they were used to only having what they could pay for, and only paying for really big, one-off purchases "on tick". It took my late grandfather, who was in his eighties when he passed, most of the last decade of his life to understand why his children and grandchildren were experiencing long term unemployment. It took him over a year to understand that my aunt, who lived in Yorkshire, *had* to use her credit card to pay for the monthly visits she made to Norfolk while my father was dying of cancer, and my grandfather was in and out of hospital. He simply couldn't grasp, for so many months, that if she didn't have a credit card, she wouldn't have been able to come. She may not have been able to be there when my father died. When my grandfather was conscious for the last time. He hadn't lived with credit cards, and therefore he believed that they were always and inevitably a terrible thing, that only "spendthrifts and gallivants" used.

Yes, some older people are just idiots who want to make other people feel bad, just like some people of any age are idiots who want to make people feel bad. But, for the most part, it's not malice, but a simple gap in lived experience, and, therefore, a gap in understanding.

Keep your patience, keep your temper, and explain, as clearly and concisely as you can, how life is for you, and the circumstances that have led to it being this way (austerity, the idea that the young and the poor are little more than livestock, rampant capitalism, the attitude of successive governments that "debt is normal", the privatisation of industry and social necessities.)

There are other "gaps", too. The gap between how we see
ourselves, and how others see us, is one that looms large when
you are unemployed, be that through simple lack of work, or
because of disability.
 For example, I see myself as a fairly average bloke, living a fairly
average life, producing averagely-decent books, making a bit of
money – not enough, but not pennies, either – from writing, which
was always my ambition, from as far back as I can remember –
married to an intelligent, funny, creative woman, with whom I am
deeply in love. I seem myself as reasonably intelligent, socially
aware, with a good grasp of economics, which comes from a
background in financial services, and a father who would happily
spend hours talking to me about anything and everything,
including things that, when I was a child, and curious about them,
other people felt were "too adult" to be discussed with someone of
my age. My father, from my earliest childhood, treated me like
an adult, and, as such, I became someone whose concerns and
fears are deeply adult concerns and fears – apparently, the
majority of British adults worry more about losing their
smartphone than Brexit. I see this as inherently childish, and a
reflection of the way society has become increasingly regressive,
trying to remain infantile forever. Because I understand the
immediate impacts of Brexit, because I can see the motivations,
hatreds, and prejudices of those behind it, because I'm good at
spotting patterns and links in events going on in the world around
me (and partly, I'll admit, because I don't actually own a
smartphone), I'm far more anxious about Brexit than I am about
losing anything, really. Things can be replaced, or lived without.
Once your rights and freedoms are gone, however, they're usually
gone for good. Once a health service is dismantled, it is rarely
rebuilt. Once entire sections of society decide it is better to kill
themselves than be killed by the policies of their government,
those people – those beautiful men and women, in whose minds
are multitudes of worlds and visions – will never be part of our
world again. I see myself as someone who is concerned about

others.

 But I am aware that pretty much everyone else sees me as a failure and a weirdo. A madman, only ever one step away from violence, with a bad case of sour grapes, because I never managed to quite live up to my potential. My concerns are seen as paranoia and "being melodramatic." My outlook and attitudes, older than my years, are seen as a sign that I'm "a fundamentally boring person." My marriage is even seen as "pointless" - because neither I nor my wife can have children.

 I seem myself as someone who expects the worst, but works for the best – other people see me as a miserable pessimist who's always moaning about something.

 It's hard, living with gaps. It's why people do crosswords – the gaps in our lives make us uncomfortable, so we fill in the gaps on a printed page, a pale effort at control.

DREAMS, MEMORIES, AND ALL INSUBSTANTIAL THINGS.

Our dreams and memories are the places where our freedom lives.

At the time of writing, the technology isn't readily available (though I'm sure it exists, somewhere) that can stop us from dreaming, or prevent us accessing and enjoying pleasant memories.

Even if you've never been employed, or have a series of short-lived attempts recorded on your CV, you'll have a memory of times when you were successful. When you won a game or marbles, or got top marks on an essay. When you learned to ride a bike, or cooked a meal for yourself for the first time. When you went on your first date, or moved into your first home. When you finally understood something that had been bewildering and frustrating you for weeks, months, maybe even years. When you saw the first shoots of something you'd planted coming up through the bare earth. When you first made someone smile. Your work isn't all of you – it isn't even most of you. Work is something you do to fill forty-five to fifty years, for half the time you're awake. Work is what you *do*; the successes you remember are what you *are*.

I'm a writer who can handle horses and dogs, who enjoys reading – books, magazines, blogs – and who prefers to spend his time in the wild, empty spaces of the world. I'm a Pagan with a genuinely Christian heart. I'm a husband, a friend.

Of all of that, I only get paid for the first thing on the list, and then not very much. I could – just about – support myself in a very basic fashion, assuming I was working every week, which, at the moment, isn't always the case, but what I earn isn't enough for holidays, household repairs, or providing for myself and my wife. It wouldn't buy new clothes. It wouldn't enable me to put a fresh coat of paint over the walls of my house, or smarten up the concrete yard that is my outside space. If my job were all I was, all I am, then I wouldn't amount to much of anything.

But I'm not just my job, not just what I get paid for. I am all the memories of the times I've succeeded, the times I've been happy. And I am my dreams – the times I *will* succeed, and be happy. I can survive almost anything, because my real life is in a place that can't easily be destroyed.

Beyond our memories and dreams, we are our principles, the things we stand for, and work to bring into greater being. When you genuinely believe in something, that belief kindles a fire that will warm you and guide you through almost anything you'll encounter.

It can take a while to work out what your enduring principles are, what you stand for, now and forever. It took me over a decade, but I finally came to understand that I stand for:

. Fairness

. Facts, accuracy, and honesty

. Realism, rather than Pollyanna-esque rose tinted thinking.

. People having a sense of humour.

That's what I live for now, and what I will fight for to my dying breath. And the last item on the list is no less important than the first – one of the greatest gifts our humanity gives us is the ability to laugh at ourselves, and realise that, in the end, we're all rather ridiculous, our concerns and preoccupations are all rather trivial. There are trees and tortoises that will outlive us, for pity's sake! In the end, you work as hard as your are able to bring about the world you want to see – but you work whilst laughing both at the world that is, and the world you want to be. Humour cures many ills, and is sometimes the only thing that keeps you going when all hope seems lost.

THE HISTORY OF UNEMPLOYMENT

Britain's distaste for the unemployed, its desire to treat them worse than a stray dog with rabies, is nothing new. It is not, whatever their other faults – and there are plenty of those to be getting on with – the sole preserve of the Conservative governments of recent years.

In the 16th century, no distinction was made between those who found themselves out of work, and homeless vagrants – both were labelled "sturdy beggars", and were branded as punishment for their first offence of "vagrancy, pan-handling, or loitering". A second offence was punishable by death.

The British have never known quite what to do with the healthy, relatively young, physically fit adults who find themselves out of work, or displaced through conflict or rogue regimes – we see this not only in Britain's current attitude to the unemployed and those with hidden disabilities, but also to the unaccompanied child refugees from Syria. They are teenagers, often teenage boys, fourteen, fifteen, sixteen, not cute little wounded infants, and so we despise them. Because support, concern, and compassion, in Britain, are reserved for the obviously frail and helpless, the child innocents. We still haven't recovered from a Victorian obsession with childhood as innocence.

The "austerity" programme of the Conservative government from 2010 onwards, with its relentless cuts to social services, support programmes, education, and health, and the endless raising of financial burdens on small and medium enterprises, has resulted in a surge of unemployed. Again, though, this is nothing new – the dissolution of the monasteries in the 1530s caused a surge in the number of 16th century individuals finding themselves destitute and at the mercy of a state without compassion. Just as the social services which are increasingly being disbanded through lack of funding previously ensured protection for those in our times who were vulnerable, and unable, for whatever reason, to fend for and defend themselves, so the monasteries of the 16th century fulfilled the same role – something that is easily forgotten in discussions on whether the Church and the State should be distinctly separate, with neither having interference in the running of the other.

While it is not within the scope of this book to discuss such things, I will say that I believe the Church should render assistance to the State in dealing with the vulnerable, the unemployed, the hopelessly unemployable, those attempting to rebuild their lives, and those who are troubled and troubling. Christians are, after all, commanded to "feed the poor" - this should be done, in my opinion, in a recognised, formal manner, in liaison with the State, and at the Church's expense. The Church, in my view, shouldn't exist to be a Sunday morning country club where like-minded people can come together to feel safe and smug. If it's there, making money (and a lot of churches, particularly large urban churches, ARE making money), it should be working with those in need – without any private agenda, or view to converting those they help to Christianity. If help is given with the expectation of church attendance and a commitment to a faith system, it is not freely given. And Christians are commanded, as I understand it, to give freely. To make believers simply by their love for one another – not by the bribery of "look at everything we've done for you..."

The monasteries didn't give completely freely, but they were open about what they expected in exchange: those they helped would work alongside the monastic community, in manual labour, which was often very physically demanding. But then, at that time, life in general was physically demanding for all but the very richest.

People who do not rely on it tend to dislike the fact that the welfare state gives "something for nothing", and, in fact, the habit of forcing claimants to do unpaid work for large chains, with no hope of a job at the end of it, isn't the best way to address the idea that welfare recipients are getting "something for nothing." A better solution would be to assign claimants to a charity, small business, or community organisation whose work was related to the individual claimant's ambitions and future plans, and who were not in a position to employ someone, but genuinely needed additional help and skills. Many, many charities and community organisations, for example, would love to have professional marketing support, but can't afford it. It is likely that there are quite a few welfare claimants who are interested in marketing, advertising, and related sectors. The claimants would gain genuine, practical work experience, the organisations would get the help they need, and, potentially, additional revenue as a result, and the wider public would perceive welfare claimants as "doing something for their money." The DWP would also no longer be dealing with a pool of claimants who were unattractive to employers because they had no relevant work experience. Everybody wins.

The welfare state itself is also not a new invention. It was not, despite what the media claim, and many people choose to believe, wrapped around the cosseted shoulders of the lower classes by a loony left-wing Labour government in the mid-twentieth century. That government, as it happens, was doing what everyone now approves of in the form of the paying of the State Pension, and the granting of free bus travel, free prescriptions, and free TV licences to the over 65s – it was trying to make life better for people who had been through hell.

The UK welfare state began its life with the 1601 Poor Law (or, to give it its full name, the Act for the Relief of the Poor.) The Act stipulated that the elderly, frail, and infirm were to be cared for in almshouses, while the physically able who were simply unable to secure employment were to be placed in workhouses, where the state would provide the materials for them to be set to useful manual labour. The children of the poor were apprenticed to trades.

Liberal people tend to react with horror to these concepts, but, certainly at that time, it was a far better option for the unemployed, and their offspring, than simply trying to fend for themselves. When young people from impoverished backgrounds are taught a skill or a trade, steps are being taken to break the cycle of poverty, which is important to bringing a country out of a death-spiral of unemployment, and a growing pool of unskilled native labour, bitterly and desperately competing with unskilled foreign labour, with the latter being preferred by employers, as they are more readily exploitable in terms of being underpaid, denied basic rights such as holiday and sick pay, and being made to work longer hours than is legal.

Unfortunately, as with many contemporary good ideas, the almshouses and workhouses were often replaced by the poor simply being given basic provisions (the "parish loaf"), as building and maintaining such establishments was expensive, just as building and maintaining shops and factories today is considered an "unaffordable" way of addressing unemployment.

In 2015, the most recent record we have available, **employment** was at its highest point since records began in 1971, at just under 75% of working age UK nationals. The mathematically-aware among you will realise that this means that just over a quarter of the eligible work force are **unemployed**. For some, this will be because of disability – but the vast majority are able to work, but unable to secure work that would pay them enough to provide for themselves and their families without further assistance from the state. Also, it is worth noting that individuals on zero-hours contracts – who don't get paid if they're "not needed" - are classed as "employed", which means that, in real terms, far more than a quarter of the working age UK national population is in a position where they do not have work that is paying them regularly.

Free market capitalism – the economic system currently operating in the UK – doesn't want full, or even near-full, employment, and will often proactively work to avoid it. There needs to be a visible pool of unemployed individuals, to act as a deterrent to those in employment to strike, or seek better pay and conditions. Unions lose power when their members fear unemployment, and free market capitalism doesn't approve of unions.

One of the biggest areas for concern at the present time is the number of people in receipt of Employment and Support Allowance (ESA), or its Universal Credit equivalent, who are "physically capable of working". The government, and society in general, have never really understood the detrimental impact of mental health issues, a fact which isn't helped by the current trend to portray a diverse and complex range of conditions, each with a unique impact on the individuals experiencing them, as something "everybody deals with from time to time", that can be magicked away by "mindfulness, good nutrition, and Cognitive Behavioural Therapy for the more extreme cases." I'm not saying that these things don't help – undoubtedly, they provide some measure of relief, and may, in fact, be all that's needed if, indeed, you're simply "stressed", or feeling "a bit down." But depression, anxiety, bipolar disorder, schizophrenia, and any number of other mental health conditions, AREN'T "stress." They aren't "feeling a bit down." The government has tried to normalise something that is inherently NOT normal, and thus has a serious and lasting detrimental impact on those who experience it. Nor is it simply a case of those with mental health issues "taking the tablets" regularly. Medication is definitely a core element in helping those with mental health conditions to become more stable, and better able to manage their condition, but medication has side effects, and, sometimes, its the side effects, rather than the condition itself, that makes work impossible.

 In the last year, I have transitioned from prescription medication to treat schizophrenia – a combination of Lamotrigine and Quetiapine, in my case, as I had a very bad reaction to Rispiridol, the most commonly prescribed anti-psychotic in the UK – to a naturopathic regime of gingko biloba, valerian, and B-complex, as the side effects of the prescription medication were having a serious impact on my ability to function. Those side effects included, but were not limited to: Lethargy, Increased sleep, Memory loss, Heightened sensitivity to light and sound (try working in the average office when you have that going on – telephones become deafening, strip lights and computer screens trigger migraines...), and haliotosis – bad breath. Not a great way to make a good impression! The naturopathic regime is much better, but not entirely without side effects of its own – I can't take pain killers, as they have extreme contraindications with gingko biloba, and the valerian causes some very vivid, very weird, dreams. But, overall, I'm more functional on the naturopathic medication than I was on the prescription variety, although it was the prescription variety that got things stable enough for me to engage with therapy, engage with researching schizophrenia for myself, and, eventually, move to the naturopathic regime. So all elements of treatment were necessary, in my case, as they are in the cases of most individuals with mental health issues. There is no magic bullet, and people and governments assuming there is is deeply damaging and unhelpful.

The numbers of people "capable of working" on ESA are not, as the media and Tories would love you to believe, the fault of overly compassionate Labour governments. It's actually down to Margaret Thatcher, who, in the 1970s, decided that a good way to improve the unemployment figures – which were shocking – was to "encourage" doctors to sign people off sick, and then move those people from unemployment benefit it incapacity benefit. Making people someone else's problem, rather than actually addressing the problem, is a long-term favourite among the courses of action open to governments.

Of course, there's more than a quarter of the working age population unemployed, because published unemployment figures don't recognise the hidden unemployed – those living off savings, and so either ineligible for welfare support, or who have chosen not to pursue it, those ineligible for JSA or Universal Credit because of care responsibilities for adult children, spouses, or elderly parents , the underemployed, who need more paid hours than they currently have, and those supported by their parents or other family, who are not looking for work because they genuinely believe they have nothing to offer. Many state schools do little or nothing to encourage self-confidence, self-esteem, and self-belief in the young people who attend, and, if those individuals are not academically talented, they all too often leave school disillusioned, and believing they "can't do anything." Britain has never been good at recognising that there are forms of intelligence and ability beyond the purely academic.

When we take all of these people into consideration, it is not unreasonable to estimate that perhaps only 50% of the eligible workforce are "fully employed" - that is, they have the hours and the wages they need to support themselves and their families without additional assistance from the state.

This could, in fact, fall even lower than 50% - remember the hysteria that erupted when the Conservatives suggested that those earning over £40,000 a year shouldn't receive Child Tax Credit? Consider the number of self-employed individuals in receipt of Working Tax Credit, because they simply can't get the income to meet all of their obligations and needs, and pay the income tax and National Insurance contributions required of them. Perhaps the number of genuinely fully employed people, who could happily get by without any financial assistance from the state, is as low as 25-30%.

Think about that for a moment. Britain, one of the richest countries in the world, could potentially have 75% of its eligible population in the position of needing to rely on state support to make ends meet – even when perhaps 50% of that 75% are in employment of some kind.

Meanwhile, big business continues to get tax breaks, and avoid the tax it is charged. Meanwhile, investment in communities, particularly those outside of London, falls every year. Meanwhile, the wealthiest are pandered to, with ever-lower tax responsibilities being asked of them.

Without full tax receipts from those able to pay, unemployment is not going to be addressed. The reliance of the employed on additional support from the state is not going to be addressed.

And, as we look to the future of employment, we see that it's only going to get worse.

THE FUTURE OF EMPLOYMENT

I recently came across a meme on Facebook that said: "Immigration isn't stealing your jobs – automation is." And it's true. Employers, as we've discussed previously, don't actually like flesh and blood employees much. We're too needy – holiday entitlement, sick pay, National Insurance contributions, parental leave, maternity leave, tea, coffee, toilet breaks, and all this on top of a salary or hourly wage! It really is too much.

Increasingly, jobs that were available for those with limited skills and educational achievement are being automated – self service checkouts, self-drive forklift trucks (and, eventually, self-drive vehicles on the roads – it's already happening in concept, the reality won't be far behind.) And it's not just low-skilled jobs that are being automated out of existence – robots are involved in microsurgery procedures, and repair of machinery, computers, and other equipment, and could eventually replace surgeons and engineers. Computers are increasingly reaching the point where they would have the capacity, with the right programming, to replace white-collar office staff. As 3D printing becomes more popular and affordable, it could easily replace human labour in the manufacturing industries. In theory, computers could even replace government, and we would be at the mercy of the coders' ideas of what is necessary and important, lawful and unlawful.

The government is encouraging and enabling this rush to technologise and automate, without any comprehension of what it means for employment of people, and, consequently, their tax revenues.

There are two potential solutions that I can see: Firstly, a universal basic income, sufficient to include a taxable element whilst still providing a reasonable standard of living, and allowing individuals to contribute to the economy through purchasing taxable items. The UK government, along with many others, are resistant to the idea of a universal basic income, believing it would "encourage idleness", without being aware that the very future they're so keen to embrace will result in *forced* ideleness.

The other option would be a shake up of the education system, and a focus on skilling, upskilling, and re-skilling individuals to work in computer programming and robotics. This could actually easily be done, as it is readily compatible with the government's current zeal for STEM (Science, Technology, Engineering and Mathematics) subjects – but it would cost the government money in the initial and mid-term phases, and the UK government can't seem to get its collective head around the idea that spending money in the immediate term often results in long-term savings. Much as they love the financial sector, they seem to have failed to learn one of the core lessons of that sector – that you have to speculate to accumulate, that it is necessary to spend money in order to make money.

The future is already kicking in the door: Uber is a transport provider which owns no vehicles. Amazon is a retailer that holds little to no inventory. Paperwork that was once processed by human beings is being man-handled into online processes, with people being cajoled, bullied, or outright forced into accepting that "it has to be done online, now." Data is handled by code crawls, even McDonalds are trying to phase out human workers and interaction where they can.

And, while traditional industries are being killed off by automation, the rage, passion, and creative ingenuity of the working class is rattling its cage, flexing its muscles, and roaring in the distance.

You are one of the 75% who are not being served by employment as it currently stands. There is an army standing with you, and for you.

The future needs to be given fully over to the working classes, because history has shown us that every societal improvement has been brought through by working class rage and frustration. And, if the powers that be aren't willing to give that future to us – then we need to find a standard to raise, and our 75% need to come together, and take it from them.

As they regularly tell us: it's for their own good.

RESOURCES AND SUPPORT

.Benefits Advice UK

www.benefitsanswers.co.uk

.Citizens' Advice

www.citizensadvice.org.uk

.Disability Rights UK

www.disabilityrightsuk.org

.Debt Advice Foundation

www.debtadvicefoundation.org

.UK Government (includes a range of information and services)

www.gov.uk

If you are in receipt of welfare, it is best to avoid raising queries and concerns with the Jobcentre or DWP if you can get the right answers and information elsewhere. The DWP have a tendency to react to any query or concern by stopping your welfare payments while they "look into the situation." Looking into a situation can take the DWP several weeks, during which time you'll still be expected to pay your rent and bills, buy groceries, have internet access, and travel to look for work and attend interviews and other appointments – all of which rapidly become difficult if you don't have money coming in.

Remember, too, to try and stay calm when you're talking to people from any of the organisations listed, or others that you know of. The person who answers the phone is usually some poor soul on minimum wage, who isn't actually able to help you – they're just there to take the details, and pass your case on to someone else. I've been that person more than once in my life, and being shouted and sworn at isn't the greatest way to spend a day. Especially not for six or seven quid an hour. If you're feeling particularly stressed and frustrated, ask to speak to a manager straight away.

Before you get in touch with an organisation, make sure you have as much information to hand as possible – financial details, bank statements, proof of ID and address if you're going into their offices, etc. It helps speed things along if you're not having to rummage around for bits of paper, or come back another time with more details.

Finally for organisations and businesses interested in creative negativity training, please email

negativeisalsoacharge@gmail.com

Defeating Worrisome Predators was brought to you by Ashley Ford-McAllister, who runs Negative Is Also A Charge, specialists in productive pessimism and creative negativity.

www.negativeisalsoacharge.wordpress.com

E: negativeisalsoacharge@gmail.com